my itty-bitty bio

Alexander Ovechkin

Cherry Lake Press

Published in the United States of America by Cherry Lake Publishing
Ann Arbor, Michigan
www.cherrylakepublishing.com

Reading Adviser: Marla Conn, MS, Ed., Literacy specialist, Read-Ability, Inc.
Book Designer: Jennifer Wahl
Illustrator: Jeff Bane

Photo Credits: © Tomas1111/Dreamstime.com, 5; © Naviya/Shutterstock, 7; © Savin Sorin Matei Contescu/Dreamstime.com, 9; © Yerchak Uladzimir/Shutterstock, 11; © Chistyakovartyom/Dreamstime.com, 13; © Jerry Coli/Dreamstime.com, 15, 17, 22; © Adwo/Shutterstock, 19, 23; © IU Liquid and water photo/Shutterstock, 21; Cover, 1, 10, 14, 18, Jeff Bane; Various frames throughout, © Shutterstock images

Cherry Lake Press is an imprint of Cherry Lake Publishing Group.

Library of Congress Cataloging-in-Publication Data

Names: Pincus, Meeg, author. | Bane, Jeff, 1957- illustrator.
Title: Alexander Ovechkin / Meeg Pincus ; illustrated by Jeff Bane.
Description: Ann Arbor, Michigan : Cherry Lake Publishing, 2021. | Series: My itty-bitty bio | Includes index. | Audience: Grades 4-6
Identifiers: LCCN 2020005724 (print) | LCCN 2020005725 (ebook) | ISBN 9781534168459 (hardcover) | ISBN 9781534170131 (paperback) | ISBN 9781534171978 (pdf) | ISBN 9781534173811 (ebook)
Subjects: LCSH: Ovechkin, Alexander, 1985---Juvenile literature. | Hockey players--Russia (Federation)--Biography--Juvenile literature. | Hockey players--United States--Biography--Juvenile literature. | Washington Capitals (Hockey team)--Juvenile literature.
Classification: LCC GV848.5.O94 P56 2021 (print) | LCC GV848.5.O94 (ebook) | DDC 796.962092 [B]--dc23
LC record available at https://lccn.loc.gov/2020005724
LC ebook record available at https://lccn.loc.gov/2020005725

Printed in the United States of America
Corporate Graphics

table of contents

About the author: Meeg Pincus has been a writer, editor, and educator for 25 years. She loves to write inspiring stories for kids about people, animals, and our planet. She lives near San Diego, California, where she enjoys the beach, reading, singing, and her family.

About the illustrator: Jeff Bane and his two business partners own a studio along the American River in Folsom, California, home of the 1849 Gold Rush. When Jeff's not sketching or illustrating for clients, he's either swimming or kayaking in the river to relax.

I was born in Moscow, Russia.
It was 1985.

My parents were **athletes**. My father played **professional** soccer. My mother was a basketball player. She has two **Olympic** gold medals.

What do you have in
common with your parents?

I grew up with two older brothers.

I always loved hockey. One of my brothers helped me practice. He died when I was 10. I was very sad. But I played in his **honor**.

What sport or activity do you love?

I became a top hockey player in Russia. I was a teenager.

ИНГОССТРАХ

The Washington Capitals asked me to play for them. The team is part of the **NHL** in the United States.

BACKSTROM
19
capitals
BAUER

I didn’t know anybody. I was **nervous**. But I made friends. I was named team captain of the Washington Capitals in 2010. I spoke only Russian.

What makes you nervous?

I helped my team win the **Stanley Cup**. This was the first time the Washington Capitals won the **championship**.

D HALL
GREAT
Challenge Cup
OCK
FAM

I worked hard. I broke many records. I hope to keep playing and to break more records.

I have come far, from Russia to the United States.

What would you like to ask me?

timeline

2004

1980

Born
1985

2018

2080

glossary & index

glossary

athletes (ATH-leets) people who are trained in or are very good at sports and physical exercise

championship (CHAM-pee-uhn-ship) a contest or final game of a series that determines the overall winner

honor (AH-nur) special respect shown for someone

nervous (NUR-vuhs) very worried about something

NHL (EN AYCH EL) National Hockey League

Olympic (uh-LIM-pik) relating to the Olympic Games, which are summer and winter contests for athletes from all over the world

professional (pruh-FESH-uh-nuhl) making money for working hard at something others do for fun

Stanley Cup (STAN-lee KUHP) the trophy awarded to the NHL team that wins the top championship

index